I0159247

Palm Lines

Che Chidi Chukwumerije

.

Also by Che Chidi Chukwumerije

Poetry Collections:
The Beautiful Ones have been born
Writing is the Happiness of Sorrow
Light of Awakening
River
Cumbrian Lines: Poems born of the Lake District
Das dauerhafte Gedicht (Poems in German)
Innengart (Poems in German)
Mmiri a zoro nwayọ nwayọ (Poems in Igbo)

Prose:
Twice is not enough
The Lake of Love
There is always something more

For children:
Somayinozo's Stories

Many thanks to Aj. Dagga Tolar and Hajo Isa
for their kind and insightful editorial suggestions.

Che Chidi Chukwumerije, Palm Lines.
Second Edition 2015
First Edition 2012 under the pseudonym Aka Teraka.
Boxwood Publishing House e.K.
ISBN 978-3-943000-70-2

Cover Photograph © Antje Renner

Che Chidi Chukumerije

—

Palm Lines

—

Poems

Boxwood Publishing House, Frankfurt.

Table of Contents

1.

The Cracked Mirror's Bottom

Alive

Alive in your grave
I hear your thoughts
Squirm
Unruffled by your
Poker mug

Two black stones
Sprout
On your grave head
Pierce my soul's louvres
Shivers me alive.

Cold come forth
I need your warmth
 - gently!
Exhume me...
With care.

Resurfacing

Your disgrace
Reflected on my bottom
Wiped with tears across your lost face
Mirrored in anguish ambushed –

Be of good cheer –
The dew
Washes the exposed leaf clean each time
The cock crows again.

Lost In The Switch

Alas! Treble now sounds
Like bass! Gold shines
Like brass! Who dulled
The taste of water?
Who turned sons into
Wailing daughters? Alas!

The wrappa moans
Look at me I am now
A pair of trousers, split in two!
Hush! Zip up your swollen lips
Cries the warrior's breastplate!
Look at ME! I am now a Bra.

There is an owl howling
Melancholy in the night
A road has split in two
Causing confusion
Because the ground has
Disappeared.

The Thirst Commandment

One man's iconolater
Is the other man's idolworshipper
Only the iconoclast
Is atheist – to some
Iconic deity itself to others
We see from different sides.

One man's woman
Some nights is another
Woman's man
– shout! all you want
Hidden things will continue
To happen in hidden places.

Understanding is
A fragment of that
Cracked mirror's bottom.
Return from your space ship
Bewildered scientist
The greater mystery is humanity.

Mixed Up

Of late I feel the surging
Of black blood in my heart
River, conqueror of artificial, man-made dams
Exploding into its original course
Of late I feel the resurgence
Of black blood through my lungs

Puzzled I gaze at my white wife, loyal pillar of love
In my heart and life... I don't understand
Baffled I gaze at my white wife walking by my side
Bringing me home and joy... I can't understand why.
A true story, unedited lifeline. How can this be possible?
Why does it grow deeper the blacker I grow?

Against all reason, against all teaching
Of the black blood within my veins
This is not what I was taught –
Yet sometimes I am everything I am not –
Eternities and mysteries locked down
Under my dense skin.

Is love a marvel, a metaphor, a quest, a riddle, a wound,
A contradiction, a miracle, an annoyance, a tempter,
Goof, spoof, proof that we never know it all, a world war,
A dark thirst, fountain of never-ending
New Beginnings, Comforter, a mystery, a teacher, a judge,
A road, a rebel, a mocker, a mirror, a moon...?

And when it seemingly ended... Blackness did not rejoice
History, culture and tradition did not exalt –
Only my heart wept heavy and light tears
Love is a mysterious path.
If you see me crying bitterly, do not comfort me
My joy is an enigmatic wonder performed by my pain.

My Father

When the rock was walking stoically
Through the mountain of time I was
On its back and thought the ground was still
Beneath my running legs –

Restless was my heart
For I felt yours beating in it
And mighty were the loud congas
Drumming out my thoughts.

Yet there is one quiet thought
Too deep to be breached
Too quiet to be heard
By any but me.

The Burden of Manhood

Morning's dues
Bog down your shoes
Drown your trails in debt
For the bow
is hungry for news
of the arrow's death.

Bearer of sorrow
What arrow, mid-flight
Can correct its course?
It is not your portion
to match
the melodious sparrow –

Tomorrow
When you have circled the sun,
it will face you:
            THE END.
Then you must be a man
And boldly strike the mark, my son -
Thine pre-ordained destiny.

The Mirror's Bottom

The mirror sang from side to side
Somewhere over the rainbow an old guitar
Picked up a young musician,
Awakened in his heart the desire
To be a Bridge.

And he is still wandering
    looking for himself –
When the masquerade dances
    not earthly drums move its feet
    but the worlds underneath.

When your heart moves
Close your ears to the *kora* you hear
Look for the mirror within
    For the mirror swings
                from side to side.

Memory of true love

Those days were magic
I was a boy but already a man
You were a woman but still a girl

We understood each other.
No matter how much they dig into our past
They'll never really understand it today

You cannot understand a fairytale
With your intellect.
  You have to be a child at heart
To understand magical love...
There is a grove
therein a cove
therein a light
therein a dove
therein a mystery.

Memory becomes an elixir.
Our hearts were broken
By the logic of separation

Perfection had to be
Enshrined
For future reference.

The sanctuary of blueprint
Guard it, a secret. A desecrated deity
Cannot be appeased by sacrifice.

Ode To Poetry

I've been biting like a volcano
Poetry has been crying lava
I've been biting hard

Stop! Stop bleeding me! Stop breaking me!
I want your nipple
Your lip, your ruthless restless tongue

Your thigh
And above it, your most tender secret
I want to reveal it, stop starving me.

The eruption was a corruption
Of merciful silence.
You should never have woken me up.

The Subtle Gift

Most things become
smaller
Receeding into
Distance.

Yet, as memories of you
Race into fargone bowels of time
Looking back all I see
You towering ever bigger in my mind –

How can this be?
Newton, Einstein and Hawkings may try
But never can explain this –
It transcends intellect.

Time, the subtle thief, with time
Has become the subtle teacher
The subtle giver
The subtle gift.

to Kwame.

Che Chidi Chukwumerije

2.

Crunchteeth of Reality

Armed Robber

The bullet leapt
Wept the barrel with
Sorrow's silent shriek protesting
The bullet's hunger

Feeding the
Blood bank's Belly, saving
Not life, but your account
Of – what? – your life?

Countless Cowries
Bagged in bloated
Human hide
Yet not enough to buy back

Recompense.

The Goodbye Bird

I quarrell with you
Proud avian
Only the strong should carry
The weak on their back!

Tell your master that.

Tell your master
Trust is no flight of mere imagination
That will rise again from its ashes
When it dips and crashes

Phoenix never was made of flesh and bone,
                              disentangled
Blood and tears have flowed into metal, mangled
Don't you know you are the one promise
That ought never be broken?

The very sky
has spat us out
in discontent!

We fail to take care of Pegasus...
Its stall's owners
SHALL PAY THE PRICE

Tell your master that!

Must we wave goodbye
To every disappearing spot in the sky?...
Ask your master that.

In memory of the victims of plane crashes in Africa

Crash

Icarus lived amongst us
Icarus did not tell us
That his wings were waxed of clay

When he flew
Our trust flew
with him!

Amadioha was certainly displeased
With this unwanted sacrifice
For wax is an insult unto the sun

Lazy clay's clumsy earthbound feet
Are not for the aquiline-hearted
Darers of higher worlds...

  He who wants safe passage
  Through heaven's corridors
  Must wash his feet Everyday.

But if tortoise continues
to borrow flight feathers
Our hearts will continue to crack

And the vampire soil will continue
to drink Black blood
Crushed in black tears.

In memory of the victims of plane crashes in Africa

Oil-drunkard

Tolotolo longa throat
Oil-drinker
I hear you coughing
Dry and raspy like a corporate copy-cat
Come, let me slap your back
Before it chokes you to death.

Your cough syrup is counterfeit
Shipped in from India or China
Fake drugs, Swiss accounts, a hundred mansions
Will not get rid of the black smoke
Stuck in your throat
So come... let me slap your back!

Last Words

A night of men ... No no no!
        Like agama flipped sideways
        his head swung spasmodically
– A man does not drink Beer WITH A STRAW! –

Armed Killers are wiping out the family
Next door to the beer and billiards parlour
They will be here next.
No, Forget the police. –

  Why do you start up?
  A real man is not afraid
  Of the loud manly shouts of
Gunshots and explosions.

If you want to help
Get up and help
  If not,
Remain calm...

Men are born to be killed
Oaks are raised to be felled
Just make sure you die for
Something worth living for –

Now drink up your beer
Pocket the black ball
Pick up your gun
Let's go defend our neighbourhood!

Ode To Quietness

Good morning, Quietness,
I remember how with surprise
I felt your absence last night.
And did I thirst for you? First I thrashed about wildly,
Clutching at every suggestion of you,

Then, exhausted, like a leopard I crouched, still,
And lay in wait for you – awake, listening,
Until the morning came… My life rolled before my inner
                                                    eyes,
Awakening you from the depths of my heart –
Good morning, Quietness, as I fall asleep at last.

Intersecular

Like a cow
Eschewing its thoughts
The worship bells
Choked my throat
Penned me to my pagy leaf

Sunday mournings
Have my sins been so many?
Stop confessing guiltily
What you profess so
Guiltlessly.

Monday is the new Sunday.
If you want to meet God,
Look for Him on Monday –
On Sunday, Saturday and Friday He is far far away,
Tired of our hypocrisy.

Corporate Eye Service

The chair
On which I am sitting
Will not stand still
I cannot
Find my footing

My mind is drenched with frenzy
My heart refuses to calm down.
That is why I stand
Beside my chair
When I am writing at my desk

One eye on the computer
One eye on the door
One eye looking out of the window
One eye at the back of my head
And one eye quietly weeping inside.

Through the window darkly I see
In another world
Palms waving frantically in the air
Like hands gesticulating desperately
For attention, for help.

Backteeth of Reality

The world rotates,
A restless insomniac,
Lays on its back
Upon its bed of thorns

The bedsheets are sweating
Blood and brine
Midnight is crying for dawn.
A dream crashes to death everyday –

What laws really govern our lives?
No constitution
No legal textbook
Can capture the reasons and dynamics of living

So why don't I stop wasting my time
With laws that terminate at death;
Seek instead for those that ever were
Ever will be.

Reincarnation Riddle

How many times do
You think you
Have lived?
  Blind mole
  I am tired of your arguments

Stray in your hole
Keep on laughing
At me –
The soft brown earth is not as thick
As my dense black skin –

  I cannot hear you.
I cannot hear you in there
Yet I know you are out there.
Your recurring epitaph
Awaits again:

The grind
Did wring you, it ground you
Pension was indeed
Your resting place.
Your nesting place.

How many times do
You think you
Have died?
  Just once more.
Just once more.

Saved By Loneliness

This morning
When I woke up
My loins were weeping
With longing for you –

Thick manly tears
Wasted on the banks of distance
The smeared silence of morning
Frustration, the fury of loneliness

Dark has been my desire
As bright as love.
Take me away
I need something stronger than hope.

That's when my spirit spoke up.
I did not know there were so many daggers
Knifed into my back
Yet I am still alive.

3.

Kissing the Palm Groove

.

Just Being I

She named me River
Because I whet her lowlands
In the hour of her drought
– I saw a palm tree
Hotly pursued by a multitude

Waving palms
But I did not understand
The power from which they sprung
Forth – must I understand?
Which sane river stops to understand itself?

Waters may rise to clouds to fall back as rain
But what woman rises from her heart to her head
To peer back down into her heart from her head
To understand herself
Without losing the misty way back to the dawn?

For she is mysterious yes it is complicated
As simple as a riddle
The flowing is the being, picture-perfect
It is frozen
Faster! Faster! Faster!

Breathlessly I never tire
The day she catches me
Is the day
She will lose her desire for me. For
She calls me River.

A Thousand Eternities

I see the sun rising
The horizon is no longer far
We have met each other halfway
The horizon is now the road.

The smell of your breast
Is a miracle
The touch of your breath
Is a poem

That ceases never to enchant
The undulating sands beneath which
My desert is overpowered
By your thousand flowers...

I am born anew
When you gently wake me up
In the night
Just to look into my eyes...

Heaven.

Heaven be your name
And though memoryless we wander
Far away in this blue grass under
The heavens,

Yet you pull me up where I see you
Calling me, reminding me, admonishing me
With your eyes in the middle
Of the night.

Heaven be our home
A thousand eternities from now
Far Beyond yonder horizon
We see.

All Or Nothing

The entire I gave
While smallness was all
She ever wanted.
But the rest of me thirsts too.

When frivolity was laughing
At its own shadow
I warned
That my heart was dripping…

When superficiality was doing the maths
Around its own tunnel vision
I insisted
My heart is dripping out…

When cunning was blind to the metaphor
Of its own despair
I fell silent
And listened to the sound of bleeding feet

Walking away.

Platitude

What is a kingdom to a God?
What is a moon to a sun?
What is thought to intuition?
What do you care?
Just dare!

When you are smashed
By your blasphemous Ambition
You will emerge
From out of the ruins of your kingdom
The shells of your broken personality...

Plant your mind
Like a budding tree
Into the deep dark soil of
Your intuition –

Let the Gardner sow
   Let the Gardner tend
        Let the Gardner reap.

That is why it took me so long
To realise we were always separating
Our love was always an ending
Never a commencing

A world is not enough for a home.
A grain of sand will do
        When love is true.

O who would have known it was a love story
When our swords first clashed?

O who would have known it was a war
When our lips first met?

And Growth.

And There Was Life

Believe unsanctimoniously
Burn robustly
Brave love. It is all we've got.

A tree dwarf
Is mightier than his tree
For his tree is but his shadow.

When you serve love
You become a master of the universe.
And cease to be a shadow.

'Tis no cliché
When God said let there be love
We heard let there be light.

Fisherman

Daily my heart weeps
My soul is drenched in a river
Flowing with thoughts of you

Of late I have become
A fisherman
Richly rewarded for my toil

Bravely diving into the lake of love
Daily my heart weeps
With joy.

Anthem

And this shall be our song, our anthem,
    That I met and did not leave you
    Although time and tide were against us
And every wind said No.

And this shall be our song, our anthem,
    That I never stopped seeking until I found you
    And my understanding of you became my guiding
                                    star
And made me stronger than every No.

And this shall be our song, our anthem,
    That nothing separates us, neither life nor death,
    Because we are in each other, path and goal,
And Heaven shall be our Yes.

Kissing In The Rain

Caked by the moon's blood
It was our virginal touch
I thought of you
As a wolf howling for mystery

As we silently
Touched without a sigh
All I remember is the look
In your observant eyes

Muddied
By the moon's blood
No rain could
Wash it away.

Dance, ye shivering droplets
Our skin is voyeur
Our dance is romance
Immortalise our first kiss.

Prey

She saw a hunter resting in the forest
His manly shoulders
Caused the trees to heave
In expectation –

She ruffled the leaves of his hair
Placed her hand on her heart
As she read his rising thoughts
He had been waiting for her.

Tremble not, lovely maiden,
Stretch out your hands and pluck
My golden fruit
For it hath not ripened in vain

This forest whispers
Told me you were
Coming…
The hunter hath found his mark.

The queen of hearts
Has met her match.
Black grass will quiver tonight
But the forest will keep our secret, my dear.

Tracing The Palm Groove

Like a glove
Her palm fit into mine
I saw her struggling
With the shock
Recognition brought.

We tried to decipher our fate
But saw neither
Its beginning nor its end
The flask has gone out of the djini
Tracing the palm groove...

Ever the palms
Lining our every path
Kissing our everything
Wild trees become a garden, untamed...
A jungle becomes a park, intriguing...

We clasp hands and become a palm nation.

Love at First Sight

She stunned me
With word
And Glare –

It took two blinks
And a hushed hiss
To realise

It was not my heart I heard
Slamming so loudly in
My ears…

It was hers.

4.

Free Spirit

Renewals

Love affairs
Whirlwind
Across the desert of loneliness...
Reassuring me that I live.

I'm grateful for every ripe watermelon,
Every mango, every grapefruit, every tangerine,
Every kiwi, pawpaw, and orange, every peach,
Ụdara, every *ube*, every *mmịmị,*

Every plum, every berry, Cherry, each date,
Every passionfruit that ever whet my appetite
Suckled on the fingers of my thirst
Stilled my restlessness.

Yet after the storm
Came always the quiet morning
Free of desire,
Full of my heart.

Standing On Society

The scar whipped
The back proudly

The ground is stepping on me
Yes I will die standing up

If you thirst for freedom, then
Feel free

Bury me standing
Up right –

Only slaves prostrate
Before their executioner!

If the ground stands on me
Well, so will I too.

The Grace

Though disgraced
I will not lose face
I will raise it
that the sun
may shine on me.

Every fibre of my being
Every corner of my soul
Every song of my spirit
Will become new –
for the flames of the sun

Have killed me.

Love Affair

When I tasted the spliff
Dragged it down to the level
Of my hungry black lips
It was a temptation it could not resist

Heavenwards it soared
With me, its quivering
Stub, on its mind
Where I met higher thoughts.

Write down
Your poems at the height
Of your madness
For after you return

You will not remember anymore
What thoughts those were
That came to you so naturally
When you were in love.

The Inner Voice

Pray you never meet
The hungry road our teachers warned us about
So lyrically you thought they were writing poems
  – They were delivering a message.

You have hair all over your body
Like an animal
But it takes more than that
To be a man.

You are sturdy
            Like a tree
  Your head is cocked and flashing
            Like the sun

  You move with charged deliberation
Like the slow swift passage of harmattan
  But it takes even much more
              THAN THIS to be a man!

So, when you listen, listen
With your inner ear
  to what the way is whispering...

So you will hear what only real men
Can see with the Inner Eye
  when the road is changing...

And then, Wayfarer, you too will speak one day
With the clear inner voice
Of a true man, safely arrived.

Frustration

I pray death
Releases me
From this torture soon

But if death be too cowardly
To leap across its shadow
Then let Life

THAT ADAMANTINE GOD
 Take me. For I am ripe
And ready to be harvested.

Every second an eternity
Every act fulfilment
Every step in finity.

Break Away

He who will change something
Must break something
Sang none other
Than the fragile little butterfly...
Wings to unwind a universe.

He who will change something
Must break something
Sang none other
Than the fragile little chicken
To the other struggling egg.

And my mother placed her burning palm
On my heart, asked me to stay...
It was balm, but he who will change
Something must break something
A generation away

Sometimes you just have to
Break away.
The hoe cracked the hearth
The sower smiled

Rebirth cracked the palm kernel of death
Death learned from rebirth
About the quest for a higher birth
The reaper smiled.

Freedom Spirit

I am on the bird's wing,
When it beats they say
It is my heart.
Where are you going,
Prodigal Son?

I am on the lion's tail.
When it twitches they say
It is my pride.
Where are you going,
Rebellious Brother?

If you put your ear
To the ground
All you will hear
Is the Spirit that
Rides within.

Crossage

Those years were a terminus
For each one of us
In all kinds of different ways...
Kwame force-fed the famished road
Folarin tip-toed o'er the dwindling bridge
Ken met a strange wayfarer who became he...

Onesi awakened from sleep into a living dream
Gee closed the window – what bird sings outside?
Feyi looked into the mirror, and cracked...
And I lost my memory
But acquired an other.
   And then we all parted ways.

Those years were a terminus
Those years of our crossing over
From boys to men
And the passage
Through the night.
'Twas the end of youth.

Defiance

How many taboos
Have you broken
As you crashed through
The jungle?

None?
Get up
And walk,
Man!

How many arrows
Have brought joy to your sorrows
Fighting the struggle
For existence?

None?
Get up
And walk,
Man!

How many battles have warmed your heart?
How many obstacles have grown you up?
Life is a shrug of manly shoulders
And an inner smile.

Defiance is but in truth
A humble bow to the life within
Before you step off
The stage.

Blue Secret Rivers

My blood is blue river today
Every thought of you beknights me
Makes me feel like royalty
For thou art my queen...

If I strode across mountains
They would prostrate before my will
Proud to be footstool
To the queen's lover

Naughty me
What a delicious secret
I feel like King Aka the Thirst
For I secretly drink from the queen's fountains

My blood is blue river today
When it runs into you
You sigh...
At night I am thine king.

Che Chidi Chukwumerije

5.

Come-Promised Land

Still Seeking The Future

I see
Wavering eyes
Tied around my ankles
Tightly beaded the masquerade stumbles

The drums think it is a dance and praise on
The familiar djini pokes his feathered skull
Out of the future – here I am!
Leaden feet leading until again

We stand on the river bank...
Sorry, where exactly?
We have been singing for the boat
Since time immemorial –

Unreversedly.

The *mamiwater*'s melodious silence answers us

Yet our ancestors did not lie
When they reassured us that the only
Real things are the invisible ones
Who refuse to see us.

If there be no boat
How shall the river
Cross us over
Onto the promised sand?

Abomination

My feet are stepping on me
My souls are brutalised
My grass is Thorn, apart

Strangers
Are laughing in glee
But my children do not understand

It is the foolish lizard
Who nods along wisely
To the snake's slithering sermon

A child slaps his father
And corrects him
Did you hear the sky fall down?

Are you not ashamed?
If it is wisdom,
Why is it vestigial?

A short tree, shorter than me
Has peed on me –
　　Can I take it like a man?

Renaissance

Water my winter
With the warm wells of your spring
Oh midnight, for dawn is near
And the other gender
Will come asking for its portion, aye
'Tis alas the stronger gender - unbeknownst to us!

Thus ride out, ride out,
Arrow of youth,
For winter is nigh!
A ploughshare went out to plough
And where it died, an Iroko grew legs
And started running south to the sea

I thought it was a river running
But the Niger is quiet these days
Silenced at gunpoint
Now the Iroko too seeks refuge over seas...
Look back! Your roots are tugging at you
Awaken from your winter sleep!

African Reverse

Verse in reverse
Who blessed my curse?
The Iroko tree
Is full of tender feelings
It's just his pride that makes him keep silent
When his children hold the axe to his face
Cut their own roots...

Where is my warrior?
Let him drop his guitar,
The bards will sing songs enough
For him in the evening
Because he freed the land from the captors,
His memory of fearlessness cured amnesia
Of the battle within...

Verse hearsed in reverse
So who blessed my curse?
An Elder has warned you
Must set forth
At the dawn the crowned crier assures us
That the sun
Yes the very sun that fell yesternight
Is standing up
Head held high proud again
A man today.
Send down the new reigns!

Once upon a future time

There are those who still
Pray with trembling lips
To the river deity,
The tree-lord strengthens
the manliness
in their blood,
The fire-being moves
Their heart and they are not
Less pious than thou!

There are those who
Resist the canon blasts
of ancestral amnesia
And for every bite of
their daily bread
Awaken the eyes in the back of their heads
And, with deep libatious heart, say
– tremulous of Hand, always –
And here, a little piece for ye too...

Nor are they less pious than thou!
For they never stepped off
the path...
Who knows what tomorrow will bring?
When the wild winds would have chased
All the deserters back home
Who knows? When, things fallen,
They hunch, apart, dejected then
In their unfamiliar ancient home

Once rejected,
   Who will
Remind them of the things of old?
Who will point with earthen finger and
Say to them? Tenderly:
Here, this is the path we were once travelling upon.
Let us, united, march on
And see what Temple
it shall lead us into.

Lineage

Look at the palm of my hand,
My lineage has run riot –
Griot! Take note!
For the palm is the root of our land.

Tapper, come down
  from them high
          intoxicating dread locks,

The Elders on the ground
Can see beyond the highest tree.
  Tapper, come down
  And tap your roots instead

Look at the palm of your land.
Before you boast, ask yourself if you really know
The back of your hand.

Remembering Africa

I dream a native hut
Was quietly at peace
With the woman inside
Forgotten within

She used to be our mother.
Briefly I met her
But her quietness is a mystery
Only my spirit can understand

Suddenly I heard the message
Of her eyes:
Only your spirit will ever understand.
Queen of home and eternity.

These Augean Stables

Let me remind people
For our memory is short –
Once we fought for independence
We thought we had snatched victory
From the jaws of defeat
But the Empire struck back.
Where are the Jedi?

The chains are invisible now
Economic, no media wasted
The jailers wear black masks now
Indigenous, anti-colonial jargon won't help
The traitors are anchored in habits
Of mentality, and you can't shoot your body
To get to your soul, can you?

The enemies of unity sleep not.
The strange Eagles are familiar Vultures
Circling overhead like puppet-masters of decay...
Seems like on the road to independence
We lost the way to self-dependence...
   Who will be ready
When the Jedi shall come?

Let me remind the people
For our memory is short –
This is not what we fought for,
Never,
These Augean stables,
This splintered map of
Caricature.

Aluta Continua

I dropped my fear
When I picked up my gun
And left the judging to God.

I breathed out
Will it be my last?
At least 'twas done with pride.

The Promised Sand

Crusted slices of solstice
Pick-pockets of time
Thoughts like a picket line
Gruelling rue in plantain stew

Crystal slivers of impotent craving
Gesticulating for the future
To hitch us a ride to complacency
Sinking in the promised sand.

The promised grass
Perfumed bush
Another generation
Another push.

The Illusion

Dead trees
blowing in the breeze
as if they were living,
yet they are dying

Foreign lands
stretching out their hands
as if they were giving.
But they are lying...

They are taking, taking back
what they lack
More than what they give –
they need More to live.

Palm Lines

—

Poems